AND SO WE COME FORTH

The Apple Family:
Conversations on Zoom

Part Two:
A Pandemic Trilogy

Richard Nelson

BROADWAY PLAY PUBLISHING INC
New York
www.broadwayplaypublishing.com
info@broadwayplaypublishing.com

AND SO WE COME FORTH

Cover photo by Jason Ardizzone-West

First edition: November 2020
I S B N: 978-0-88145-888-6

Book design: Marie Donovan
Page make-up: Adobe InDesign
Typeface: Palatino

Why Now?
Notes on theater right now.

The director Peter Book was once asked the question, 'What is the future of theater?' Without a moment's hesitation, he replied: 'Tell me, what is the future of food?'

In the middle of huge social upheaval, civil unrest, deep seated injustice, as well as a shattering, devastating world-wide pandemic, which has caused economic chaos and widespread personal tragedy, why put on a play?

When the world feels so profoundly uncertain, why do theater?

With the theaters themselves closed, and theater artists out of work and predicted to be some of the last workers to be re-employed, with theater institutions folding and furloughs commonplace, with anger and demands for social justice and an end to racism within the profession itself causing fissures and confusions, is this really the moment for plays?

Let's say one even finds the time, and resources, and outlets to do some sort of play; when there are no theaters open, no live audiences, no person to person rehearsals, what sort of play do these times require, if any? Does theater have a role in a world that is in so much flux, anguish and pain, in protest, and facing profound uncertainty?

Or does it have a responsibility? Maybe even an opportunity?

There are of course different ways to answer these questions; there are many examples of theater being a rich, and sometimes entertaining, expression of protest and ideologies themselves, with theater makers putting to work the full range of their theatrical tools for a specific cause. At other times, theater has also been a seemingly necessary escape from a troubled world; a momentary respite from the conflicts raging outside its walls.

Theater also can be something else entirely.

There is a theater that chooses not to be a participant on the battlefields, but rather something running parallel to them. This theater does not attempt to portray the arguments being waged, nor does it allow itself to become a platform for these arguments, but rather portrays characters who are simply trying to understand the world they are in, our world—as they ask themselves and each other: who they are, where they fit in, where they belong, do they matter. While all the time, these characters just try and live their lives, which are complicated and complex, perhaps more so than any of the arguments circling around them. A theater that is about *trying to understand,* as opposed to one *with answers. A theater made up of questions and questioning.*

Whenever I find myself lost, either as a playwright or person, I turn to Anton Chekhov for help. Here's what I found in a letter he wrote to a friend, "I am not a liberal, nor a conservative, nor a gradualist, nor a monk, nor an indifferentist. I wanted to be a free artist and that's all…I hate lies and violence in all their forms… Hypocrisy, dim-wittedness and tyranny reign not only in merchants' homes and police stations…I look upon brands and labels as prejudice. My holy of holies is the human body, health, intelligence, talent, inspiration, love, and the most absolute freedom, freedom from violence and lies, however the two manifest themselves."

The motto of the Comédie Française in Paris is: "*Simul et Singulis*". To be together and to be alone.

In part, this sums up the essence or at least the ambition of my kind of theater: to bring together *strangers*, sit them in the dark, and have them grow together into a group; that is, to come 'together' while being 'alone'. When together, they find themselves with other human beings, who also have families, brothers and sisters, also have problems that are universal, truths that are multicultural. There in the dark, watching theater together, perhaps they will come to feel, if only briefly, that they are not alone.

Here can be a good reason to do a play in very difficult times: to share that in our confusions, in our questioning, in our self-doubts and self-questioning; we are not alone.

A program note to a play I wrote during the tumultuous 2016 election, seems relevant today:

"In troubled and troubling times, theater has not only an opportunity, but the responsibility, to portray the confusion and articulate the ambiguities, doubts, and fears of its time. The goal then being not to argue a side or a point, but to attempt to portray people and worlds as they are, not as we wish them to be. Theater, to my mind, is not an argument, but an effort to create and portray human complexity, which we then share with a living audience, human being to human being."

R N

Published in The Guardian *28 June 2020*

AND SO WE COME FORTH was first produced
by Apple Family Productions on its own dedicated
YouTube Channel on 1 July 2020, with the following
cast and creative contributors:

RICHARD APPLE...Jay O Sanders
BARBARA APPLE.................................. Maryann Plunkett
MARIAN APPLE...Laila Robins
JANE APPLE .... Sally Murphy
TIM ANDREWS... Stephen Kunken

Director... Richard Nelson
Production stage manager ....Jared Oberholtzer
Technical director.. Ido Levran

For Apple Family Productions:
General manager ....Rebecca Sherman
Production manager .... Jeff Harris
Press representative .... Candi Adams
Company manager .... Anna Wheeler
Photographer.................................. Jason Ardizzone-West

Apple Family Productions is supported by Susie
Sainsbury.

NOTE

I use a single quotation mark to notate when the character is paraphrasing, and double quotation marks when the character is actually reading from a source.

CHARACTERS & SETTING

In Rhinebeck, New York:

RICHARD APPLE, *lawyer in the state's Governor's office; lives in Albany, staying with his sister,* BARBARA.

BARBARA APPLE, *his sister, high school English teacher.*

MARIAN APPLE, *his sister, elementary school teacher.*

JANE APPLE, *his sister, free-lance writer for local magazines.*

In Brooklyn:

TIM ANDREWS, JANE's *partner, manager of a Rhinebeck restaurant and part-time actor, lives in Rhinebeck, staying with his ex-wife, Diane.*

Time: A day in early July, 2020. 7:30 P M-9 P M
Place: Four computer screens:

Locations in Rhinebeck, New York:

BARBARA *and* RICHARD *appear in the dining room of* BARBARA APPLE's *house on Center Street, Rhinebeck, where* RICHARD *has been staying for months.*

JANE *appears in the living room of her and* TIM's *apartment on South Street, Rhinebeck.*

MARIAN *appears in the living room of her house on Platt Street, Rhinebeck.*

Location in Brooklyn:

TIM *appears in the living room of Diane's apartment.*

To Larissa

1.
Take-out and Cereal.

(On one screen: BARBARA *sits waiting. She looks at herself.)*

(Second screen, an empty living room.)

(After a moment, RICHARD *appears behind* BARBARA.)

*(*RICHARD *leans over and looks at the screen:)*

RICHARD: Where'd she go?

BARBARA: To take the dog out.

RICHARD: You want the chicken tikka by itself or with some of the saag paneer?

BARBARA: One at a time is fine…

*(*RICHARD *continues to look into the screen. He hums.)*

BARBARA: I don't care… She's not there, Richard.

RICHARD: I can see that. I'm looking at her apartment…

BARBARA: It's okay. A bit messy. But that's always been Jane…

RICHARD: Yeh… *(He continues to look and hums.)*

BARBARA: I'm going to ask you to name that. What you're humming. *(She 'copies' his tuneless humming.)*

RICHARD: It's not anything, Barbara.

BARBARA: I know. It's not music.

*(*JANE *appears in her screen.)*

JANE: *(As she puts on her headphones)* He didn't do anything, Max. *(She looks at herself in the screen.)*

BARBARA: Maybe you rushed him.

JANE: I didn't rush him, Barbara. Tim's not on?

RICHARD: Not yet…

BARBARA: Marian said she wanted to take a shower. She was working in her garden all day.

RICHARD: She does that a lot now. She stands out there all day.

JANE: Good for her. Leave Marian alone.

RICHARD: *(To* BARBARA*)* Do we want a tablecloth?

BARBARA: I don't care.

RICHARD: Then maybe we don't need one. *(As he goes:)* And you don't want them together, the chicken and the spinach? *(He goes off.)*

BARBARA: Anything. *(Calls, repeats)* I don't care. *(To* JANE*)* Should I put on a tablecloth?

JANE: Why are you asking me?

BARBARA: I've got one right here… *(She has gotten up to get a tablecloth nearby.)*

JANE: Why bother?

*(*JANE *looks at herself in the screen. Fixes her hair as:)*

BARBARA: *(Off)* We got take-out from Cinnamon. *(She returns and puts on the tablecloth:)*

JANE: I know. Was there anyone else there?

BARBARA: At Cinnamon?

JANE: Outside at the tables… Are people really doing that?

BARBARA: One couple, Richard said. He picked up curbside… They're hanging in. I know them, they won't give up…

(BARBARA *sees* RICHARD *approaching with plates of Indian food:)*

BARBARA: Thank you, Richard. Thank you for 'cooking'.

RICHARD: You changed your mind about the tablecloth. You want the candles?

BARBARA: No, Richard. And if I do, I'll get them. Just please, sit down.

RICHARD: *(To* BARBARA*)* You have everything?

BARBARA: Just sit down. Jane, what are you eating?

RICHARD: *(As he sits)* This is a dinner, Jane.

JANE: I know. I'll get mine... *(She doesn't get up.)*

RICHARD: *(To* BARBARA*)* Can we open the wine?

BARBARA: I left the bottles in the mudroom. *(Before* RICHARD *can get up)* I'll get the wine. *(To* JANE*)* I've started keeping them out there... *(She goes.)*

JANE: I'd do that if we had a mud room. We just wash our bottles and line them up on the kitchen counter. Must look like all we do is drink.... *(Then)* You started to tell me about your house...

RICHARD: It's not my house yet. Get your dinner. We're eating dinner together. Do you even have a dinner?

JANE: All right. All right... *(She gets up.)*

RICHARD: I could have brought you take out.

(MARIAN *appears on a screen.)*

MARIAN: *(A joke)* Am I the first?

(As BARBARA *passes behind* RICHARD *with a wine bottle:)*

BARBARA: No, Marian... You're not the first. *(She heads off to the kitchen.)*

MARIAN: That would have been a change.

RICHARD: Yeh.

MARIAN: *(Getting settled)* So did you see your house?

RICHARD: It's not my house. Not yet.

MARIAN: And?

RICHARD: Where's your dinner? I left it on your porch.

MARIAN: I'm warming it up.

RICHARD: It's warm. [his plate:] This is warm...

MARIAN: *(Over this)* And what did you think?

(JANE entering with a bowl:)

JANE: About what?

MARIAN: Did Barbara go with you? *(Answering JANE)* His house on Livingston.

RICHARD: No, she didn't.

MARIAN: You should have let her go with you, Richard.

RICHARD: I can look at a house by myself...

MARIAN: She knows everyone.

RICHARD: Why does that matter?

(BARBARA returning with two glasses of wine, having heard:)

BARBARA: He wanted to go by himself. Do it all by himself.

RICHARD: I liked the house.

MARIAN: Better be quick.

JANE: *(To BARBARA)* Do I know which one?

BARBARA: With the empty lot? Between Parsonage and Beech?

JANE: Oh I know that.

BARBARA: *(Over this)* They're selling the lot too. Both together. So two lots.

MARIAN: That's rare.

BARBARA: *(Over this)* Brand new kitchen. Brand new back porch. New bathrooms. They just did a big renovation.

JANE: Why'd they do that?

RICHARD: Barbara, you didn't see it.

JANE: *(Ignoring him)* Then why are they selling, Barbara?

MARIAN: Are they flipping?

BARBARA: They're New Yorkers, it was their weekend place. Then suddenly they sell their apartment in Manhattan, take all that pile of money and they've put a bid on the Frost house on Chestnut. I guess they're now going to live here.

MARIAN: The big wraparound porch, Jane.

JANE: I love that house.

MARIAN: Too big for you, Richard.

BARBARA: So they needed more than a weekend home, I guess. He worked in T V. Works. Maybe retiring now?

RICHARD: *(To BARBARA)* How do you know this?

MARIAN: *(Obviously)* Becky.

RICHARD: So what did I think of the house, Barbara? Did I like it?

BARBARA: How would I know, Richard? *(To her sisters)* I think he did.

MARIAN: *(Noticing)* Are you eating cereal, Jane?

BARBARA: Don't you have any food?

JANE: I have food.

(TIM appears on a screen; he has a beer:)

TIM: Sorry.

RICHARD: *(Over this)* Tim.

TIM: Richard. Barbara. Marian. Jane...

JANE: *(Over this)* Hi. Hi.

TIM: *(To JANE, over this)* I was doing the dishes.

JANE: Did you already eat?

TIM: I'll have dessert with you...

JANE: *(Over this)* Why did you eat?

TIM: I had no choice.

MARIAN: My dinner should be warm by now... Excuse me... *(As she goes:)* Tim, Jane's eating cereal.

JANE: Stop it.

(Then)

TIM: Why are you doing that?

RICHARD: I offered to get her take out.

BARBARA: Indian from Cinnamon.

TIM: *(To JANE)* You like them.

JANE: I'm fine. I like cereal. It's easy. *(Changing the subject)* You okay? You do look tired.

TIM: I'm okay.

JANE: You want to go to bed?

TIM: I want to be here...I want to be there.

(Then:)

RICHARD: How's Brooklyn?

TIM: It's good....

RICHARD: *(To BARBARA)* There's the naan in the bag...

BARBARA: *(To RICHARD)* Maybe we should have warmed up ours.

RICHARD: Mine's warm. *(Points off, to* BARBARA*)* And there's that green and that red sauce…. I can bring it out…

BARBARA: *(Over the end of this)* I'll get it if I want it…

(As MARIAN *is returning with a plate:)*

RICHARD: Tim, Marian now has a 'gentleman caller'.

MARIAN: Is that what you're calling him? I like that.

TIM: I've been gone two days.

BARBARA: *(To* RICHARD*)* Rhinebeck has turned you into such a gossip.

RICHARD: You two talk about it all the time.

MARIAN: About my gentleman caller?

TIM: Who is he?

JANE: He walks by her house with his dog. *(To* MARIAN*)* What? Like five times a day, right? That's what you said.

MARIAN: At least. But who's counting?

BARBARA: And she's outside gardening. Tim, now she gardens. In her *front* yard. A lot.

TIM: Who is—?

JANE: You don't know him.

BARBARA: *(Smiles, to* MARIAN*)* And tell Tim what you wear.

TIM: What?

BARBARA: Tell him.

MARIAN: Nothing special. Shorts. Halter top…

JANE: Tim, halter top…

BARBARA: Who gardens like that?

(Blackout)

2.
Karen and her Friend.

(The same. Short time later. In the middle of conversation, as they eat:)

JANE: *(To* TIM*)* Did you give Karen my present?

TIM: I did.

JANE: And did she like it?

TIM: She hasn't opened it. She's opening presents tonight. With her friends on Zoom. My daughter has organized a big thing on Zoom—her own late graduation thing. A lot of her class—she said they can go into groups somehow—. Called 'rooms'.

RICHARD: That never works for me...

MARIAN: Jane, what did you give her?

JANE: For graduation? A dress of mine. Karen and I are the same size. Sundress. The yellow and white with the straps that cross in back...

MARIAN: You loved that dress. You still wear it.

JANE: I know...

BARBARA: Maybe Karen will wear it tonight on Zoom.

RICHARD: That would be nice.

JANE: Tell me if she does.

TIM: I will.

JANE: Don't make her.

TIM: I couldn't.

MARIAN: How's your ex doing?

BARBARA: She has a name, Marian. Diane.

JANE: Can she hear? Is Diane there?

TIM: In the kitchen... And I have headphones.... She can't hear. You can now say whatever you want about her.

JANE: *(A 'joke')* So now's my big chance...

MARIAN: And her husband?

TIM: He watches T V.

MARIAN: The actor.

JANE: Tim says, he's not that good of an actor, Marian.

MARIAN: Is he the one who kept getting the parts that you wanted?

TIM: You told her that? That was years ago, Jane. He's not a bad guy. He used to be very funny... Great story teller, waiting for auditions... But you don't want to be an actor right now... Not in the theater... I feel sorry for him.

JANE: *(A 'joke')* You're still on the couch?

TIM: I'm on the couch. She's got a husband. Who's here.

(They eat.)

TIM: Jane, there are still some of the same pictures on the wall. From way back... Things I bought. It's been so strange...

JANE: You're coming back tomorrow?

TIM: Of course I am.

JANE: And if Karen wants you to stay longer...?

TIM: She doesn't... I want to come home...

JANE: Good. I'm glad.

TIM: She thinks my daughter has me wrapped around her little... *(Finger)*. Has Jane said that to you?

(They eat.)

TIM: *(To* JANE*)* It's not true. Come on.

JANE: Tim's ex has been hinting that she'd like us to take Karen for the summer.

BARBARA: You told us.

JANE: Is she still hinting that?

TIM: Jane, Diane's now come right out and asked.

JANE: You're kidding. She did?

TIM: Just now over dinner.

JANE: Shit.

TIM: I haven't agreed.

JANE: I certainly hope you'd want to talk to me first—

TIM: I am.

(Then)

JANE: I see…

BARBARA: She knows the size of your apartment? Your ex.

TIM: Karen's stayed with us… I'm sure she's told her Mom.

JANE: Oh I'm sure her Mom asked.

(They eat.)

JANE: What does Karen want?

TIM: She certainly doesn't want to move to Rhinebeck…

RICHARD: What's wrong with Rhinebeck?

BARBARA: Richard…

RICHARD: I know. I was joking.

BARBARA: Her friends are there…. And Rhinebeck isn't Brooklyn…

RICHARD: *(To* BARBARA*)* Oh I didn't realize that.

MARIAN: If I were eighteen I wouldn't want to be here. Not now.

TIM: Jane, she just says she really needs a break.

JANE: Your ex?

TIM: Yeh. And there's the classmate… It's too much right now she says. So she asked. Begged me, actually… I'd never heard Diane like that.

JANE: What do you mean, the classmate? What are you talking about?

TIM: She'd have to come too, Jane. The classmate.

JANE: Tim—

TIM: Before you say anything…

MARIAN: Let him explain.

BARBARA: Leave her alone, Marian.

JANE: What 'classmate'?

TIM: Maggie. Maggie's been staying here with them. Maggie, that's her name. She sleeps in Karen's room. She's been here for a few weeks now. I hadn't known why. I thought maybe her parents were on a trip?

RICHARD: In a pandemic?

TIM: I didn't really think about it, Richard. Then last night Diane says she wants to tell me why Maggie is here… And how it's not been her choice…Maggie's a sweet girl, Jane.

(Then)

JANE: So…? Why is she there?

TIM: Diane explained all this to me. A few weeks ago my daughter is home and Maggie calls her. Maggie's parents are screaming at each other in the background. And Maggie's crying and then she says on the phone:

'Karen, do you see the lightning? There's lightning, Karen.' And it's a sunny afternoon.

JANE: I don't understand.

TIM: Diane said that was their code…

BARBARA: Maggie's safe word, Tim.

TIM: That's what Diane called it too.

BARBARA: That's what's it's called. I'm a school teacher. *(To* RICHARD*)* A safe word is—.

RICHARD: *(Over this)* I know this, Barbara.

TIM: So Karen runs to her mother, *(Quietly)* and you know what Diane's like. Not the most pro-active…

JANE: No. No…

TIM: *(Quietly)* "Are you sure? Is it really our business?" Karen finally convinces her that something bad is happening to her friend. But Diane doesn't know what to do: 'Call the police? And they do what? Talk to the parents? Take the girl away? To where? There's a fucking pandemic.' *(Then)* So Karen gets her step-dad to walk over to Maggie's house with her, just a few blocks away. And they can hear the fight from the street. Maggie runs out of the house, crying and shouting, 'Let's go. Let's go, please…' *(Then)* Diane called Maggie's parents, to tell them where their daughter now was. So they wouldn't worry? And— this, this says it all, Diane says…

JANE: What?

TIM: The mother is relieved, just glad that Maggie is out of their house… *(Then)* Maggie would have to come too. They could both stay in our spare bedroom.

JANE: That's my office…

TIM: They're staying in the same bed now. So they could do that with us… *(Then, sort of changing the subject:)* Richard, Diane asked me if I'd teach my daughter how to drive while — if she's up here.

RICHARD: Rhinebeck's a good place to learn. It's not the city...

TIM: *(Over this)* Karen said she didn't want to learn to drive a car... She's only ever going to live in a city.

(JANE suddenly stands.)

JANE: Fuck!

TIM: What? Where are you going?

JANE: Max wants to go out again.

TIM: You don't have to take him out every time he—.

JANE: He didn't go the last time. I don't want him peeing in here... *(As she goes off:)* He's your dog.

TIM: *(Calls)* I'm in Brooklyn.

BARBARA: If your daughter doesn't want to come to Rhinebeck, Tim... And I can understand that.

TIM: I can too. But she can't stay with her mother anymore. *(Almost a whisper)* This apartment here has gotten very tense. *(Then)* Why is she eating cereal?

(No response)

TIM: Did you meet up today?

BARBARA: Who?

TIM: All of you. Jane told me this morning that you were getting together in Barbara's back yard. This afternoon.

RICHARD: We did. We got together. It was nice.

BARBARA: It was. Six feet apart.

MARIAN: Tim, they still doing that there?

TIM: Not really. And Jane came? This afternoon.

BARBARA: She didn't feel like it.

TIM: Is she getting out?

BARBARA: She walks the dog… So she has to get out. *(Then)* Richard, what if the girls could stay here with us?

RICHARD: His daughter doesn't want to be here… You heard Tim.

BARBARA: Tim, you know how we love Karen. How much Benjamin enjoyed her when he got so sick…

TIM: I do remember that…

RICHARD: *(To* BARBARA*)* And where would you stay? Or where would I stay?

BARBARA: I don't know…

TIM: We'll work it out, Barbara.

MARIAN: Could we get into trouble, bringing Maggie up here to Rhinebeck?

BARBARA: What do you mean?

MARIAN: Richard, would it seem like kidnapping?

TIM: She's eighteen years old.

RICHARD: Tim, have her parents even been told?

TIM: Diane said she's already called Maggie's mom. Who just kept saying, 'you know, we're not like this… This is not us…' Once or twice, it seems, Maggie just got smacked, got in their way… Got between them… The mom said, they hadn't meant to hurt her…

MARIAN: Jesus…

JANE: *(Coming back:)* He must have heard something outside. False alarm. I think he just does that for attention.

TIM: You weren't gone very long.

JANE: He didn't have to go. *(Back to the previous conversation)* Tim would that even be safe?

MARIAN: What?

JANE: Karen and her friend here.

MARIAN: Maggie.

JANE: *(To* MARIAN*)* It doesn't matter what her name is. Where has she been? Where have they both been? Your daughter too. Do you know?

TIM: I don't know, Jane.

(Then)

JANE: Are you going to find out?

TIM: I'm sure they've been out… Jane, people are now starting to get out. Everyone's not you.

JANE: You mean as careful as me.

TIM: Yes. That's what I meant.

JANE: I'm just asking if they have they been careful? Can I ask that? Have they been really careful?

TIM: I don't know that. You want me to ask?

JANE: Yes.

TIM: So what's 'really careful?'

JANE: Come on, Tim.

TIM: I'll ask. But will that make any difference, Jane?

JANE: I don't know. I don't know…

(Blackout)

3.
Questions.

(The same, a short time later. In the middle of conversation, as they continue to eat:)

BARBARA: I sent the invitation to Billy…

MARIAN: He told me.

JANE: You talked to him?

MARIAN: We FaceTimed. He was happy to get it, but he thinks he can't join us tonight.

BARBARA: I didn't think he would—.

MARIAN: He said he wanted to, Jane.

JANE: My son's very busy...

MARIAN: Jane, he got a haircut. The girlfriend's getting better... She's really learned to use those clippers you sent them, Richard...

BARBARA: *(To* RICHARD*)* You bought those for your hair... He doesn't need clippers...

MARIAN: Jane, he didn't know Tim was in Brooklyn.

JANE: I didn't tell him...

MARIAN: *(Over this)* He asked if you were all right.

JANE: What did you say?

MARIAN: *(Over this)* With Tim being away.

JANE: What did you say, Marian?

MARIAN: That Tim's back tomorrow. And we're all just down the street. *(Changing the subject from* JANE*)* Barbara, they don't need any more masks. Billy said, they have enough... The girlfriend's two aunts have been sending masks too. I didn't know.

JANE: Emily. Her name's Emily.

MARIAN: *(Continues)* Barbara, Billy said our masks are better.

BARBARA: He's just saying that.

MARIAN: I don't think so.

JANE: Marian, you told him I was fine?

MARIAN: Yeh. Of course.

JANE: I don't want my son worrying about me.

TIM: He's your son.

MARIAN: *(Changing the subject)* Barbara, she's been baking bread. Emily.

BARBARA: Everyone's baking bread. There's no yeast anywhere... Tops. Hannaford.

MARIAN: I asked him for a photo of 'Emily's bread...'

BARBARA: I'd like to see that too.

MARIAN: She's not a baker.

JANE: I really don't want him to worry about me, Marian.

MARIAN: I told him you were just fine.

(As they eat:)

MARIAN: He told me something....

JANE: Billy?

BARBARA: Today?

MARIAN: That I keep thinking about... A story he said he'd heard Uncle Richard tell...

RICHARD: What story...? What?

BARBARA: *(A joke, to* RICHARD*)* Uh-oh...

MARIAN: About Grandma, in the seventies, I think. Walking down 125th Street.

RICHARD: Oh that.

TIM: Do I know this?

JANE: I know it. *(To* TIM*)* I don't think so.

BARBARA: *(To* RICHARD*)* When did you tell him that?

TIM: What story, Marian?

MARIAN: Tim, Grandma told this on herself.

RICHARD: She did.

MARIAN: Bless her. She gets off the train at 125th and walks west. This is way before Harlem had a hint of gentrification. And she walks along, you want to tell it, Richard? She walks along and she hears a voice say, 'Whitey you ought to go home.' *(Then)* She keeps walking, a little faster. 'Whitey you ought to go home.' A hand touches her shoulder, she shudders, and she turns, and there's a black man and he's saying, 'Lady, you dropped your comb.' And he hands her, her hair comb that had fallen out.

RICHARD: *(To* BARBARA*)* She told that on herself.

MARIAN: He said he'd been thinking about that...

BARBARA: I'm sure.

TIM: Of course... Sure.

JANE: Richard, why was Grandma on 125th Street?

RICHARD: There'd been a fire in the tunnel into Grand Central. So everyone had to get off and walk across town to the subway. I don't remember telling Billy that.

BARBARA: He probably overheard it, Richard... Marian, did Billy say anything else? About that story?

MARIAN: No.

RICHARD: Just that he's been thinking about it...?

MARIAN: Right... He's been thinking about it.

RICHARD: And wanted us to know that.

MARIAN: I guess. He brought it up.

(They eat.)

JANE: Neither of their jobs is going to come back.

RICHARD: Billy and Emily's?

JANE: Nobody's said anything to either of them, but he's convinced himself of that...

RICHARD: He could be wrong, Jane.

JANE: And those in his office who still have their jobs—the loan money is going to run out any day, he said. So that will push Billy even farther away from getting his job back...

MARIAN: He doesn't seem that worried though, Jane.

JANE: Maybe he's gotten used to disappointment, Marian... Even expects it.

BARBARA: I hope that's not true.

MARIAN: Richard, he thanked us for the help... The deposits went through.

JANE: He should write you both.

RICHARD: He doesn't need to thank me. I'm his Uncle.

TIM: Jane and I would help him if we could...

BARBARA: We all know that.

(Then)

JANE: Billy and Emily told me something funny.

TIM: What?

RICHARD: *(To* BARBARA*)* Good, something funny.

JANE: *(Over this)* They said, the hardest hit among their friends, during the worst of the lockdown? Were those hoping to date. You know, looking to date...

RICHARD: How do you date in a pandemic?

BARBARA: Right.

JANE: They said, you know how it used to be a pretty big thing—a statement—when you went to bed with someone...

RICHARD: Not that big of a statement.

BARBARA: Depends, Richard.

RICHARD: Not in Albany.

JANE: *(Over this)* To sleep together. But with the virus — the big step… It'd become — when do you hold hands…?

TIM: That's probably all changed now… They're out now…

JANE: I'm sure… But it's funny to think about…

BARBARA: We do adapt… Don't we? *(An example)* Tim, Marian's been splashing the bored little kids next door to her with the hose…

TIM: Good for you.

MARIAN: It shoots more than six feet, especially if you put your finger on the nozzle. It's summertime.

BARBARA: *(Another:)* Billy's girlfriend and—

TIM: Emily.

BARBARA: —I have been sharing music suggestions.

JANE: You told me. That's nice.

MARIAN: *(Same time)* I didn't know that.

BARBARA: She doesn't know a lot about sixties music.

RICHARD: And you do?

BARBARA: I do, Richard. I had an adolescence. I didn't just study law. *(Continues)* I don't know if she's humoring me.

TIM: I doubt it.

JANE: Probably.

BARBARA: She seems interested, Tim.

MARIAN: My friend Hannah has been trying to convince me to start in on Animal Crossing.

TIM: Don't go there. It's an endless pit.

MARIAN: She started with her grandkids. Everyone is playing it she said.

BARBARA: Richard plays it.

TIM: I can't believe that.

BARBARA: *(Over this)* He 'loves' Animal Crossing.

RICHARD: With my daughter. Something we've done together online, Barbara... Like twice.

BARBARA: Richard's daughter told me something funny when we were talking the other day...

RICHARD: What?

BARBARA: We have secrets too. She's my niece. *(Smiles)* She said she can tell right away when she's zooming with a friend who's now living with their parents.

JANE: How can she tell?

BARBARA: There are photos on the wall—in *frames*. *(Laughs)*

(They eat.)

BARBARA: I reached out again last night to a couple of my former students.

JANE: What about this time?

BARBARA: You know, the same. I've told you. What it was like when I was in college. What we went through then. What *we* were doing then. How upset our parents got. I thought that might, you know....

MARIAN: What?

BARBARA: Maybe make a connection? Start a conversation?

I don't know what I wanted. But then one of them wrote back, 'Don't make this about yourself, Barbara'.

TIM: That's harsh.

BARBARA: It hurt me, Tim.

TIM: Of course.

BARBARA: My old students have always been interested in what I had to say. Always before. And I am always very thoughtful about how I say things to them. I think about how I put things. I think I've been thoughtful and careful... *(Then)* Tim, two of my closest former students did text, the last couple of days, and asked me not to write again for a while. They didn't need 'advice' right now. I wasn't giving them 'advice.' I was trying to talk to them. 'Let's just pause this for now, Barbara,' one texted back... For Christ sake...

(Short pause)

RICHARD: This is changing the subject. Is that okay?

(Others shrug.)

RICHARD: One of my closest friends up in Albany... In the Governor's office. A very nice guy. Good lawyer. *(Then. Smiles, new thought)* He tells me, all the bureaucrats are watching the politicians promise everything under the sun right now... And they're just shaking their heads... Taking bets on how long this will last...Albany. *(Then)* Anyway, my friend's college roommate recently died. This is what I wanted to tell you.

TIM: Of Corona—?

RICHARD: I think so. I assume so. Two months or so ago. My friend hadn't seen him for years. Then last week he gets a call out of the blue. *(He stands and pours himself water from a pitcher on a nearby table.)*

BARBARA: You told me this.

RICHARD: But I haven't told them. *(Continues)* The man's two sons; they'd found their Dad's address book, and saw my friend's name in Albany,

BARBARA: Pretty close to Catskill...

RICHARD: Sort of. And the sons are desperate. *(Then)*
They'd already sold their Dad's house, they have to get
out, they've been cleaning it, throwing lots away into a
big dumpster that's in the front yard. The dumpster's
going to be carted away tomorrow.

BARBARA: And they couldn't change that?

RICHARD: That's what he said, Barbara. *(Continues)*
So the sons are now asking my friend: 'what do you
think we should do with all of Dad's stuff in his study?
We're about to throw it away, but then thought maybe
we better ask someone... '

BARBARA: It's a good thing they asked.

RICHARD: He'd been a poet. Their Dad. He'd started
off as something else in college in the sixties. But he'd
gotten into everything 'sixties', and so gave up pre-
med and became a poet. Never became famous, but he
had been part of a pretty famous circle, my friend said.
The Andy Warhol world.

TIM: Really? Warhol?

RICHARD: Wrote for Warhol's magazine, wrote poems.

BARBARA: He helped with the films, you said.

RICHARD: Did I? Then he did. So my friend drops
everything, puts on a mask, drives to Catskill. And
the poet's study is—untouched. Even cigarette butts...
A bottle of whiskey with just an inch left. And boxes
and boxes and boxes of papers, notebooks, letters from
people he worked with or interviewed or just friends.
He named a few; I recognize some, Hunter Thompson,
Norman Mailer.

BARBARA: He found a poem hand-written by Warhol.

RICHARD: I was about to tell them that.

BARBARA: —with a drawing... The sons were about to
throw all of it out.

RICHARD: Neither are in the Arts, I think in business.

BARBARA: That happens, doesn't it? From one generation to the next...

RICHARD: They had no idea who their Dad was... And so for the next ten hours, my friend, racing against the garbage men, saves what he can, boxes up what he's saved, and leaves the rest to the dumpster... He's going to see if SUNY Albany wants any of the stuff...

BARBARA: I'm sure they will, Richard. I told you that.

RICHARD: He calls me and tells me all this last night...

BARBARA: What could have been lost... And what probably was.

RICHARD: He did his best, Barbara.

BARBARA: I'm sure he tried.

RICHARD: He's a lawyer, not a poet.

BARBARA: He could have asked me.

RICHARD: He doesn't know you, Barbara... An entire man's life nearly tossed into a dumpster.

JANE: You having second thoughts about retiring, Richard?

MARIAN: I wondered the same thing.

RICHARD: That's there, I'm sure. That's part of it, but pretty much everything, to me, now feels up in the air. And unreal. Unsettled. Uncertain. And there's the worry, isn't there, that anything and everything could end up in that fucking dumpster... Barbara, where's the email we got this morning? I printed it out.

BARBARA: Yes, we should show them that... On my desk...?

(As RICHARD goes to the desk.)

JANE: You still print out your emails?

RICHARD: *(From a distance)* I still like touching things, Jane. Here it is, Barbara. From Masha. Our friend in California. We've known her for years...

MARIAN: Your Russian friend?

BARBARA: That's her, Marian...

RICHARD: *(To* BARBARA*)* Here... Read it to our sisters and Tim. She's a very smart woman.

MARIAN: I remember her well. Very interesting.

RICHARD: A bit older than us. A good person.

BARBARA: *(Reads)* "Dear Barbara and Richard, We are worried about everything that is happening. Howard is stoically calm—

RICHARD: Her husband.

BARBARA: "— but I know that this is the surface. He has to maintain his reputation of a good WASP. I am out of my mind with grief. I'm Russian." *(Then)* "This morning Howard recited to me Lincoln's Gettysburg Address. And I burst into tears." *(Then)* "It is an impossible time. I have never felt more lost. Have you? Really lost. I tell Howard the internet has a lot to answer for. He says it's exposed all kinds of things that need to be known. And he's right of course. But when everybody starts keeping an eye on everybody else hoping to catch an awkward word or phrase and report it to—authorities. I have been there. I have lived that."

RICHARD: She grew up in the Soviet Union.

BARBARA: "Am I going back to that? I thought I had left all that behind." *(Then)* "Anyway, how are you both? Do you feel any of this too? And bravo to your nephew's friends who were arrested."

JANE: You told her about Billy and his friends?

RICHARD: We did.

BARBARA: "We can only hope that these marches
achieve something. But I do wonder: when? When?
'And that—is the question.'" She teaches Shakespeare.
(Then) "To amuse ourselves and pass the time, which
seems endless now, Howard and I have made up a
game which we play over cocktails. We take turns
asking each other questions, only questions, no
answers are allowed. Somehow that feels just right for
now. *(Then)* Should you be interested, here's a list of
the questions from last night." *(Then)*
"What kind of country should we have?
What kind do we have?
What kind can we expect it to become?
What we do knock down, or pull down or blow up?
What do we ignore?
What is left to learn from?
Who gets a pass?
And why?
Is there happiness? That was Howard's, I told him it
was stupid.
What do you miss most?
How do you spend your days?
Do we go out or stay in?
What is the most important thing your child should
know about you?
Do you care?
Do you listen?
Do you dream?
Do you remember your nightmares?
Does truth exist anymore?
Should I just get out of the way?
What have we become?
What will happen?
And will we understand anything more when it does?
We've made it a rule to stop after our third drink..."
(Then. Reads) "Howard and I sent this set of questions
to a younger friend and she wrote back without

even looking at them, saying that you shouldn't be asking questions right now. So please, keep them to yourselves. Or if we must, if we really must question right now, do it only with very close friends, and only in the privacy of one's home." *(She folds up the email. Then:)* Anyway, life goes on. Yesterday I went to the dentist. The first time out of my town in three months. Now there are outdoor tables at restaurants on our main street; with flowers in vases. So things are slowly coming back. Or do you think that won't happen now?

TIM: That's another question...

(Lights fade.)

4.
Hope and Fear.

(The same; a short time later. In the middle of conversation:)

RICHARD: *(Defending himself, to* BARBARA*)* Tim likes history.

BARBARA: Richard...

TIM: I do. What?

BARBARA: Tim, I told him he should do a history of Albany. He knows Albany. He doesn't know Rhinebeck. *(To* RICHARD*)* You haven't lived here.

JANE: He's buying a house.

RICHARD: Tim, take your cemetery.

BARBARA: It's not his cemetery.

RICHARD: Where you and Jane have been taking walks...

BARBARA: *(Standing)* I'm done. Who wants ice cream? I want ice cream. Marian?

MARIAN: You offering to get it for me? We're not in the same room. We're not in the same house.

BARBARA: Do you have any?

MARIAN: I'm not hungry, Barbara.

BARBARA: Did you eat? Show me...

MARIAN: I have to show you my plate?

BARBARA: *(To* RICHARD*)* She hardly ate...

MARIAN: I'll have leftovers.

TIM: We have ice cream, Jane.

JANE: I finished it last night, about two in the morning.

TIM: You're not serious. Two in the morning?

JANE: Your dog licked the carton... Ask him.

RICHARD: *(Back to his story)* Tim, take your small cemetery, that's just sitting there on the edge of the village.

(BARBARA *has sat back down.)*

BARBARA: 'Just sitting there.' Where's it going to go, Richard?

RICHARD: *(Ignoring her, begins a list)* There's a Vice President buried there.

MARIAN: Of what?

RICHARD: The United States, Marian. What do you think I'm saying?

MARIAN: Barbara, did you know that?

RICHARD: *(Over this)* Two senators. Congressmen... *(Amazed:)* Rhinebeck. *(Continues to list)* Daisy Suckley, she's there.

TIM: Who's—?

RICHARD: *(Over this)* Who by many accounts was Roosevelt's mistress for a while… Also a distant cousin.

JANE: *(Over the end of this)* Do we really know that?

RICHARD: I think we do. I do.

BARBARA: People at Wilderstein resent that, Richard.

RICHARD: And then, Tim, here is the killer—

BARBARA: *(mocking)* 'The killer.'

RICHARD: *(Ignoring her, over this)* — not that far away, a hundred yards maybe—Lorena Hickok's grave.

MARIAN: I'm sorry, who's Lorena—?

RICHARD: Marian, how long have you lived here?

BARBARA: Longer than any of us, Richard.

RICHARD: She was very likely, by many accounts—

BARBARA: More 'accounts'.

RICHARD: *(Over this)* —*Eleanor* Roosevelt's lover, Marian. And so—over here you have Franklin's…

BARBARA: 'Over where?'

RICHARD: And over there you have Eleanor's —. I'm thinking of calling the chapter 'the Cemetery of the Mistresses'.

BARBARA: People here aren't going to be very happy with that, Richard.

JANE: So you have decided to write the book?

RICHARD: 'A biography of Rhinebeck.'

BARBARA: Not just a history, a 'biography'.

RICHARD: The first one, first history of Rhinebeck, Tim…

TIM: What?

RICHARD: Was written in the 1890s. You know who wrote it? *(Then)* A retired lawyer. The mistresses are buried so close together — Hickock could just wave at Daisy.

BARBARA: You told me Hickock was cremated.

RICHARD: She was.

BARBARA: And left on a shelf for ten years at Dapson's Funeral Home.

RICHARD: About ten years. *(To the others)* That's another story.

BARBARA: So how's Hickock going to wave at Daisy, if she was cremated? Wave with what?

RICHARD: It's a figure of speech. Actually, Tim, I'm thinking of—.

BARBARA: Maybe he's heard enough.

RICHARD: I thought you were getting ice cream. *(Continues)* Tim, Thomas Wolfe wrote a big chunk—

BARBARA: 'big chunk.'

RICHARD: *(Over this)* of *Look Homeward Angel* in Rhinebeck. Barbara didn't know that, and how long have you lived here? Tim, just this morning I found this online—a Prince Obolensky, he married an Astor girl. And they lived for a while here in Rhinebeck. He was a Russian Prince. Poor but married well. He claimed that he was a direct descendent of Genghis Khan. *(Amazed again)* Rhinebeck…I don't know where I'll fit that, Barbara. More wine? *(He gets up to get wine.)*

BARBARA: No, thanks. Tim…?

JANE: Why is everything to Tim?

BARBARA: He's been away.

JANE: Two days.

BARBARA: Tim, I have a Richard story.

(This stops RICHARD.*)*

BARBARA: I just remembered it this morning.
Something reminded me of it.

RICHARD: What story? *(He sits back down without getting
wine.)*

BARBARA: When I found that arrowhead in our
backyard, Richard. Jane, Marian, you were too
young. I was about eleven. And boy was I excited. An
arrowhead. In our own backyard. And our parents
were excited. Everyone wanted to see it. To know how
I'd found it. What it felt like to find it. How old it must
be. And my brother here, he must have felt a little...

RICHARD: What did I feel?

BARBARA: Guess. *(To the others)* So he trades some
of his baseball cards? To a friend whose father has a
collection of—arrowheads. So Richard in a trade gets
some of those, stolen by his friend from his father.
And then without telling anyone, every day Richard
goes out into our yard and comes back with, guess
what— 'I've found an arrow head!' Every day... 'I've
found another one.' Everyone forgot about mine...
They just kept admiring his fucking arrowheads. His
even had numbers in ink on them... They were from
a collection! Richard said that's what the Indians did,
they numbered them... Mom and Dad didn't even
question him...

(Short pause)

RICHARD: Why are you saying this? I don't understand.

BARBARA: I've lived in this village, Richard, for twenty
years. I live and work here. Please, stop telling me
about it.

(Then)

RICHARD: I'm just—.

BARBARA: Enough. *(Pause. She finishes her wine.)*

RICHARD: Now you want wine...?

BARBARA: Sure. Thank you. In the fridge...

RICHARD: I know where it is... *(He goes off.)*

(Then)

BARBARA: We're fine...

(Then)

JANE: *(To* TIM*)* Does Karen know what she's doing about college? Is it happening?

MARIAN: Who knows?

BARBARA: No one knows. About anything.

TIM: Last I heard, she's thinking about taking a gap year now. A lot of her friends are thinking about that.

JANE: And living where?

TIM: I know...

JANE: If she's not welcome at home...

TIM: It's not a question of being 'welcome'—.

JANE: We did try this once before, for a year. And it was difficult.

TIM: She was younger then, Jane...

JANE: But you said she doesn't want to be here.

TIM: *(Quiet)* They can't stay here.

JANE: And she doesn't want to live in Rhinebeck. So why wouldn't it even be worse?

TIM: Jane...

JANE: Can we even afford it?

(Then)

MARIAN: Jane, Kate, who lives down the street?

JANE: Kate. I know. What about her?

BARBARA: Who lives with Rose, the dancer, Tim.

TIM: Right, that Kate. What?

MARIAN: She sent out an email. One of her E S L students, a boy from Mexico. He'd just arrived in early March...

TIM: Bad luck... Early March.

MARIAN: And he was staying with his aunt, but she got really sick. She's now in the hospital. So Kate's written to ask if anyone could—take the young man for a while...? Take him into your home. *(Shrugs)* He's obviously been exposed... Maybe has it and doesn't know. He's fourteen. I guess now on his own. Doesn't speak English. Doesn't drive of course... *(Then)* No one's offered to take him. It's hard for everyone...

(RICHARD returns with wine for him and BARBARA.)

BARBARA: That took a while.

RICHARD: I was looking out the window at your lovely yard...

(Then)

BARBARA: I'm sorry.

RICHARD: No. No reason to be, Barbara... *(Then)* Everyone, I doubt if Barbara has told you—.

BARBARA: What now, Richard?

RICHARD: *(To BARBARA)* I've been helping you.

BARBARA: What?

RICHARD: She's been asked to make a little video—.

BARBARA: Oh that. I'm giving up on that, Richard.

TIM: What video?

RICHARD: *(To BARBARA)* What did you think I was going to say?

BARBARA: Go ahead, you can talk about Rhinebeck.

MARIAN: Tell us about the video, Richard.

RICHARD: For her students, Marian. The students who've just graduated—

MARIAN: The ones still talking to you.

RICHARD: (*Over this*) They're all doing videos—.

BARBARA: They didn't get a graduation.

RICHARD: (*Over this*) —each their own thing. And some of the teachers are doing them too.

BARBARA: (*To* RICHARD) The students aren't going to want to watch our videos. They've heard enough from us. From me. It's time to shut up.

RICHARD: That's not what you've said.

BARBARA: Richard—

JANE: What has she said?

RICHARD: That she's not going to just walk away and shut up.

(*Then*)

TIM: Will it be on their own special YouTube Channel?

BARBARA: I don't know that, Tim.

TIM: That's a nice idea, Barbara. And it's easy to set up.

BARBARA: A bunch of us said we'd try…

MARIAN: So what's your video going to be?

RICHARD: We're working on that, Marian.

BARBARA: Marian, what do you say? What can you say to these kids right now? It all sounds so obvious, when you say it. And unnecessary… Why do it, Richard?

RICHARD: (*Ignoring her*) This morning we wrote some very close friends. To get a broader sense of things… We got the idea from Masha. Different kinds of people.

Maybe something they wrote would inspire…? That's what we thought, right?

BARBARA: You did.

JANE: You wrote them what, Richard?

TIM: I was going to ask that.

RICHARD: Our own bunch of questions, such as: 'What do you fear?' 'What do you hope for?'

MARIAN: Did anyone write back yet?

BARBARA: We just wrote them, Marian.

RICHARD: *(To* BARBARA*)* A few already have answered…

MARIAN: Anything so far that's interesting…?

RICHARD: To me, Marian. I don't know about the students… *(To* BARBARA*)* They're interested. *(Reaching for a paper)* Here…I've started printing them out…

JANE: You know you don't have to…

TIM: It's okay, Jane.

RICHARD: *(To* BARBARA, *trying to hand her the paper)* You want to read…?

*(*BARBARA *doesn't take it.)*

BARBARA: You do it.

RICHARD: We're doing this together…

BARBARA: I know.

RICHARD: This was…here. This one. He—fears for the country. The divisions. He fears the police. He really fears the election… And what happens if he wins… *(Reads)* 'It's a mess.' 'I am so tired of feeling isolated…'

JANE: We all feel this.

RICHARD: *(Reads)* "I hope that I am still relevant when it's time to go back to work."

BARBARA: He's my age.

RICHARD: Then he adds: "actually that's not a hope, it's a fear." And then, and we love this—

BARBARA: What? (*She looks:*) We do. Listen. Listen to this…

RICHARD: Here is his hope: 'I hope—I am wrong.'

(*They laugh.*)

RICHARD: (*Another:*) This one was hard to read…

(RICHARD *shows* BARBARA, *she nods.*)

RICHARD: I know her well and I didn't see this coming. She doesn't really answer the question—

BARBARA: But she does… In her way, Richard.

RICHARD: She's a literature professor, very smart.

BARBARA: I went to school with her.

RICHARD: It's a paragraph. (*Reads*) "Everything I've been thinking about as possible future work, doesn't seem necessary anymore. Imperceptibly, these times have changed my view of things. I looked at some Proust this morning: brilliant, interesting, lively and somehow…totally useless and dated, yes, dated. Faulkner's prose is wonderful. But I no longer feel any curiosity. I know that art doesn't save. That in practical terms it is always 'useless'." (*Then*) "And that has been fine with me. But now I feel disoriented; something I always thought was important no longer seems so important, something has changed. There now is such a great sense of urgency, but for what? Where will it end?"

BARBARA: I got a call this morning. My writer friend in Rhinecliff. (*To the others*) We'd written him these questions. (*To* RICHARD) He didn't want to write the answers down. He wanted to talk. I think he really needed to talk. (*Then. To everyone*) He told me—he

wakes up most days with furies all around him.
'Furies', he said, like those in Greek plays. Somehow,
on good days, he finds the will to turn these furies,
and the thoughts they bring, into lines of dialogue for
characters to speak. 'When I do this,' he says, 'it's as if
I have exorcised my fears, or at least the worst of them.
And of course only for a while.' 'To create characters',
he said, 'who speak my fears and express the loss I face
every morning — my hope is to continue doing that.'

(Short pause)

MARIAN: I was lying in the bath last night. And it just
occurred to me, I all of a sudden realized: I have not
touched another human being for over three months.

BARBARA: Marian...

MARIAN: It's true. It's true. Not a hand. A shoulder. I
haven't even been bumped by someone in the grocery
store... We're that careful. We've been told to be.
(Smiles) I suddenly realized there in my bathtub: this is
what I'm missing... And so *this* is why I'm feeling the
way I feel... *(Then)* Thank god it's summer. If this had
been the fall, and it was getting darker and colder...I'd
go mad. *(Then she reaches out and puts her hand up to
the screen with her palm and fingers:)* This isn't the same
thing. This is not touching...

(Then)

RICHARD: So what does Barbara say to her kids in her
video? Anything? *(Then)* No suggestions?

(Short pause)

TIM: I should probably be a good guest and see if Diane
wants the computer...I'm hogging it... She always
used to complain about that.

JANE: Go if you have to, Tim...

(TIM doesn't move.)

BARBARA: Tim, when Karen was here last, she was a real help to me with Benjamin. Remember that, Marian?

TIM: Oh I do. She entertained him.

BARBARA: And he her... Though I don't think he knew who she was...

JANE: Maybe not.

BARBARA: He did keep asking her name. "I'm Karen, Uncle Benjamin. Tim's my father."

JANE: "Who's Tim?"

BARBARA: He was always saying that. 'Who's Tim?'

TIM: Oh I remember that.

RICHARD: Me too. 'Who's Tim?'

JANE: I think he knew. He just did that.

BARBARA: Karen was very, very good with him. She'd sit with him for hours. Read him stories... We'll make her happy. And her friend. We'll make it a family project...

RICHARD: That would scare me off.

BARBARA: Be quiet.

MARIAN: Tim, she never met Evan.

(Then)

TIM: No. She never did...

MARIAN: (A list) We'll make her masks... She can come by and stand in the street and I can spray her with the hose.

JANE: She's eighteen years old, Marian.

MARIAN: So what? I sprayed Richard last week.

RICHARD: You did...

BARBARA: We didn't have dessert. The ice cream.

RICHARD: I'm not hungry….

BARBARA: So we're winding down?

RICHARD: I'm full.

(Then)

MARIAN: We don't want to go. I almost said 'go home.'

TIM: Diane did say very pointedly: 'don't stay on too long.' *(whispers)* I need to get home…

(No one moves.)

MARIAN: We're not moving…

(Laughter)

BARBARA: All I have to do is push a button and you're gone… Just like that. *(Then)* Some of my students, before the end of the school year, they asked me for a summer reading list. I doubt if they're reading anything now. But they did ask, even those who were graduating, so it wasn't about—.

RICHARD: Sucking up.

BARBARA: They don't suck up.

RICHARD: I'm not sure about that.

BARBARA: *(Over this)* So I thought about it. And—I said maybe it's a good time to read up on the Renaissance. You know, a new beginning.

TIM: That's not going to fly now, Barbara. The Renaissance.

RICHARD: No…

BARBARA: I know. I know. Anyway, I suggested this. And one of the teachers heard about my reading list. She suddenly remembered that her young son had gotten 'a fridge magnet kit' for Christmas and had never even touched it. She found it in a closet, completely unused. And so to do something, I guess, she started making some.

MARIAN: Fridge magnets??

BARBARA: And now she's giving them out to other teachers. Drops them off in mailboxes, to those of us in the village. She's in the village. She left me mine. On it is written: *(Then)* "And so we come forth—to behold the stars." *(Then)* It's the last line of Dante's *Inferno*. He says that the moment he walks out of hell… 'And so we come forth to behold the stars.' Right now it's on my fridge…

(No one knows what to say.)

TIM: *(Looks off, whispers)* Diane's now staring at me. *(Calls, off)* I'm getting off… *(To the others)* I've got to go. She wants her computer. She's making this gesture… *(Gestures typing on a computer.)* I'll see you tomorrow.

JANE: Can't wait, Tim.

TIM: Me too.

BARBARA: Say hi to Karen and congratulations on graduating. Or whatever… Say whatever…

MARIAN: And from all of us. Whatever…

TIM: Goodnight.

OTHERS: Goodnight…

TIM: *(To JANE)* Love you.

JANE: Love you too, Tim.

TIM: Stay safe…

JANE: You too. *(A joke)* Stay on the couch…

(TIM signs off.)

BARBARA: I think we're done. Unless you're going to eat some more food, Marian.

MARIAN: I'm done. I ate.

JANE: I ate all my cereal...

BARBARA: *(Picking up)* I've got it, Richard. Sit. *(She picks up.)*

RICHARD: So you have a gentleman caller, Marian.

MARIAN: Or stalker. I guess right now that's the same thing. *(Then)* Let's keep doing this.

RICHARD: Hopefully not for too much longer.

MARIAN: I didn't mean just the Zoom, Richard...

RICHARD: I know that.

MARIAN: Jane... Hug... *(She gestures that she is hugging JANE.)*

JANE: I hug you back... *(She gestures that she is hugging MARIAN.)*

RICHARD: You all right, Marian?

MARIAN: I'm fine. Thanks for the Indian food. Who paid?

BARBARA: Richard.

MARIAN: He can afford it. I'll have it for lunch too. You staying on, Jane?

JANE: Just for a second.

MARIAN: Goodnight all.

JANE: Night.

RICHARD: Night.

BARBARA: Marian... It's garbage night...

MARIAN: Oh, don't I know. Can't wait. Goodnight everyone...

BARBARA: Take care...

(MARIAN signs off.)

RICHARD: *(To* BARBARA*)* She'll be fine… *(Getting up)* I'll do the dishes. *(To* JANE*)* You're going to stay for a while?

JANE: For a minute.

RICHARD: I'll say goodnight now…

JANE: Night, Richard.

RICHARD: Tim's back tomorrow…

JANE: Oh I know.

RICHARD: Night, Jane… *(He goes off to the kitchen.)*

BARBARA: It's complicated, I know. I can imagine. Karen and Maggie here…

JANE: You read my mind. I want to be a good person.

BARBARA: Jane…

JANE: It's going to be so hard…

BARBARA: I know. And Tim knows that. You will make it work. And we'll help. You're not alone.

JANE: When Marian said that…about not touching a human being.

BARBARA: I know… For three months, Jane. I know…

JANE: What have we done to ourselves?

BARBARA: You asking me?

JANE: *(Laughs)* No. No, I'm not.

BARBARA: *(Laughs)* Good! Because I don't know. Let me play something for you… *(She reaches for her smart phone.)*

JANE: *(Suddenly stands up)* Damn it…

BARBARA: What?

JANE: Max needs to go out…. Shit, you don't do that inside! Bad dog… You are a bad dog. Barbara, I should go. I have to clean this up. I'm sorry. We'll talk tomorrow. I really need to keep talking.

BARBARA: Me too. Me too.

JANE: It seems to help.

BARBARA: I know. It does.

JANE: Night!

BARBARA: Night…

JANE: *(Over this)* Bad dog! Fuck. You wait until Tim gets home… *(She signs out.)*

(BARBARA is alone.)

(She fiddles with her smart phone, finding a piece of music, and plays it:)

(Mozart's Soave Sia Il Vento *from* Cosi Fan Tutti. *[3 minutes])*

(RICHARD returns.)

RICHARD: *(Picking up her glass)* Done? *(She nods.)* Jane's gone. *(She nods.)*

BARBARA: *(About the music)* Tim told me he sang in this opera in school… He's a trained singer, you know.

RICHARD: I know.

BARBARA: I like to sit in my backyard and listen to this. And just shut everything out… For a few minutes. Is that wrong? To shut things out?

RICHARD: Sometimes we have to, Barbara…

BARBARA: The two characters are singing about when they'll be back with their loves… Back together… And when will that ever be?

(RICHARD starts to go.)

BARBARA: Richard?

RICHARD: *(Stops)* What, Barbara?

BARBARA: I don't think I have ever felt this old.

RICHARD: Turn it up, so I can hear it in the kitchen…

(BARBARA *turns up the music.*)

(*She catches her face in the screen.*)

(*Continues to listen to the music*)

(*Then another look at the screen*)

(*She looks at herself.*)

(*The music finishes.*)

(*She signs off.*)

END OF PLAY

*9 7 8 0 8 8 1 4 5 8 8 8 6 *